Published simultaneously in 2002 by Helen Exley Giftbooks in Great Britain and the USA.
20 19 18 17 16 15 14
Selection and arrangement copyright © Helen Exley 2002.
The moral right of the author has been asserted.
ISBN 978-1-86187-428-3
A copy of the CIP data is available from the Brtish Library on request. All rights reserved.

No part of this publication may be reproduced or transmitted in any form or by any means, electronic or otherwise, without permission in writing from the publisher.
Words and pictures selected by Helen Exley.
Printed in China.
Helen Exley Giftbooks, 16 Chalk Hill, Watford, WD19 4BG, UK.

TIMELESS VALUES

A HELEN EXLEY GIFTBOOK

Principles are eternal....

WILLIAM JENNINGS BRYAN (1860-1925)

The hallmark of courage in our age of conformity
is the capacity to stand on one's convictions —
not obstinately or defiantly
(these are gestures of defensiveness, not courage)
nor as a gesture of retaliation,
but simply because these are what one believes.

ROLLO MAY (1909-1994)

YOU ARE WHAT YOU ARE BY WHAT YOU BELIEVE.

OPRAH WINFREY, B.1954

To have a purpose that is worthwhile,

and that is steadily being accomplished,

that is one of the secrets of a life

that is worth living.

one of the secrets of life

HERBERT CASSON (1869-1951)

...I AM BOUND TO LIVE UP TO WHAT LIGHT I HAVE

I am not bound to win

    but I am bound to be true.

I am not bound to succeed

    but I am bound to live up to

      what light I have.

ABRAHAM LINCOLN (1809-1865)

THE GREAT THING IN THIS WORLD
IS NOT SO MUCH WHERE WE ARE,
BUT IN WHAT DIRECTION
WE ARE MOVING.

OLIVER WENDELL HOLMES (1809-1894)

The only real satisfaction there is, is to be growing up inwardly all the time, becoming more just, true, generous, simple, manly, womanly, kind, active. And this we can all do, by doing each day the day's work as well as we can.

JAMES FREEMAN CLARKE (1810-1888)

I BELIEVE THAT WORK IS LOVE IN ACTION. IT IS MY FEELING THAT IF MORE PEOPLE THOUGHT ABOUT THEIR WORK AND THEIR LIVES IN THIS WAY, THEY COULD ACCOMPLISH SO MUCH.

JEANE PINCKERT DIXON (1918-1997)

take your heart to work

Integrate what you believe
into every single area of your life.
Take your heart to work
and ask the most and best of everybody else.
Don't let your special character and values,
the secret that you know
and no one else does, the truth –
don't let that get swallowed up
by the great chewing complacency.

MERYL STREEP, B.1949

THE ONE PREDOMINANT DUTY
IS TO FIND ONE'S WORK AND DO IT.

CHARLOTTE PERKINS (1860-1935)

*Do continue to believe that with your feeling
and your work you are taking part in
the greatest; the more strongly you cultivate in yourself
this belief, the more will reality and the world
go forward from it.*

RAINER MARIA RILKE (1875-1926)

I SLEPT AND DREAMED THAT LIFE WAS JOY,
I AWOKE AND SAW THAT LIFE WAS DUTY,
I ACTED, AND BEHOLD: DUTY WAS JOY.

RABINDRANATH TAGORE (1861-1941)

*...a basic decency
and goodness*

Each person has inside a basic decency and goodness.
If he listens to it and acts on it, he is giving a great deal of what
it is the world needs most. It is not complicated
but it takes courage. It takes courage for a person to listen
to his own goodness and act on it.

PABLO CASALS (1876-1973)

*Just be what you are
and speak from your guts and heart —
it's all a person has.*

HUBERT H. HUMPHREY (1911-1978)

You're all you've got

Don't compromise yourself. You're all you've got.

JANIS JOPLIN (1943-1970)

I WOULD BE TRUE

I would be true, for there are those who trust me;

I would be pure, for there are those who care;

I would be strong, for there is much to suffer;

I would be brave, for there is much to dare.

I would be friend of all – the foe, the friendless;

I would be giving and forget the gift;

I would be humble, for I know my weakness;

I would look up – and laugh – and love – and lift.

HOWARD ARNOLD WALTER (1883-1918)

Work hard, play often and live in love.

STUART AND LINDA MACFARLANE

Duty does not have to be dull.
Love can make it beautiful and fill it with life.

AUTHOR UNKNOWN

Gentleness is a divine trait:
nothing is so strong as gentleness and
nothing so gentle as real strength.

RALPH W. SOCKMAN (1889-1970)

My feeling is that there is nothing in life
but refraining from hurting others,
and comforting those that are sad.

OLIVE SCHREINER (1855-1920)

Most of what I really needed to know about how to live,

and what to do, I learned in kindergarten....

These things I learned. Share everything. Play fair.

Don't injure people. Put things back where you found them.

Clean up your own mess. Don't take things that aren't yours.

Say you're sorry when you hurt somebody. Wash your hands

before you eat. Learn some and think some; draw and paint,

sing and dance, play and work everyday some.

When you go out into the outside world, watch for traffic.

Be aware of the sense of wonder....

The Golden Rule is Love....

Think of what a better world it would be if we all had a basic policy

for our nation and other nations – to always put things back

where we found them and clean up our own mess.

ROBERT FULGHUM, B.1937

Our fathers gave us many laws, which they had learned from their fathers. These laws were good. They told us to treat all people as they treated us; that we should never be the first to break a bargain; that it was a disgrace to tell a lie; that we should speak only the truth....

CHIEF JOSEPH (1830-1904)

*Do what you believe in and believe
in what you do.
All else is a waste of energy and time.*

NISARGADATTA

What does it matter how one comes by the truth
so long as one pounces upon it and lives by it.

HENRY MILLER (1891-1980)

INTEGRITY RINGS LIKE FINE GLASS. TRUE, CLEAR AND REASSURING.

PAM BROWN, B.1928

*Truth makes the face
of that person shine
who speaks and owns it....*

ROBERT SOUTH (1634-1716)

Dare to be true

No pleasure is comparable to the standing upon the vantage-ground of truth.

FRANCIS BACON (1561-1626)

A reputation for good judgment,
for fair dealing, for truth,
and for rectitude, is itself a fortune.

HENRY WARD BEECHER (1813-1887)

May we find a way to meet the task

Mighty causes are calling us – the freeing of women,
the training of children, the putting down of hate
and murder and poverty – all these and more.
But they call with voices that mean work and sacrifice
and death. May we find a way to meet the task.

W.E.B. DU BOIS (1868-1963)

To awaken each morning with a smile
brightening my face; to greet the day
with reverence for the opportunities it contains;
to approach my work with a clean mind;
to hold ever before me, even in the doing
of little things, the ultimate purpose toward
which I am working; to meet men and women
with laughter on my lips and love in my heart;
to be gentle, kind, and courteous
through all the hours; to approach the night
with weariness that ever woos sleep and the joy
that comes from work well done
this is how I desire to waste wisely my days.

THOMAS DEKKER (C.1570-1641)

REAL JOY COMES NOT FROM
EASE OR RICHES OR FROM
THE PRAISE OF MEN,
BUT FROM DOING
SOMETHING WORTHWHILE.

SIR WILFRED GRENFELL
(1865-1940)

ALL THE GREAT THINGS ARE SIMPLE,

AND MANY CAN BE EXPRESSED IN A SINGLE WORD:

FREEDOM; JUSTICE; HONOUR; DUTY; MERCY; HOPE.

SIR WINSTON CHURCHILL (1874-1965)

simple, great things

The best things are nearest — breath in your nostrils,
light in your eyes, flowers at your feet, duties at your hand,
the path of Right just before you.
Do not grasp at the stars, but do life's plain common work
as it comes, certain that daily duties and daily bread
are the sweetest things in life.

ROBERT LOUIS STEVENSON (1850-1894)

to think quietly,
to act gently...

To live content with small means; to seek elegance rather than luxury, and refinement rather than fashion; to be worthy, not respectable, and wealthy, not rich; to study hard, think quietly, talk gently, act frankly; to listen to the stars and birds, to babes and sages, with open heart; to bear on cheerfully, do all bravely....

WILLIAM ELLERY CHANNING
(1780-1842)

I believe...

I believe in the eternal importance of the home
as the fundamental institution of society.

I believe in the immeasurable possibilities of every boy and girl.

I believe in the imagination, the trust, the hopes and ideals
which dwell in the hearts of all children.

I believe in the beauty of nature, of art, of books, and of friendship.

I believe in the satisfactions of duty.

I believe in the little homely joys of everyday life....

OZORA DAVIS (1866-1931)

IT'S NOT WHAT YOU DO ONCE IN AWHILE,
IT'S WHAT YOU DO DAY IN AND DAY OUT
THAT MAKES THE DIFFERENCE.

JENNY CRAIG

I believe that all of us
have the capacity for one adventure inside us,
but great adventure is facing responsibility
day after day.

WILLIAM GORDON,
EPISCOPAL BISHOP OF ALASKA

Try not to become a man of success.
Rather become a man of value.

ALBERT EINSTEIN (1879-1955)

Focusing our attention —
daily and hourly —
not on what is wrong,
but on what we love and value,
allows us to participate
in the birth of a better future,
ushered in by the choices
we make each and every day.

CAROL PEARSON

What we love

HOW ONE LIVES IS,
AFTER ALL, ONE OF THE RIGHTS
LEFT TO THE INDIVIDUAL —
WHEN AND IF ONE HAS
THE OPPORTUNITY TO CHOOSE.

ALICE WALKER, B.1944

and value

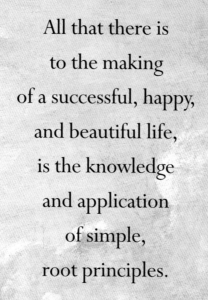

All that there is
to the making
of a successful, happy,
and beautiful life,
is the knowledge
and application
of simple,
root principles.

JAMES ALLEN
(1849 - 1925)

This is what you shall do: love earth and sun and animals, despise riches, give alms to anyone that asks, stand up for the stupid and crazy, devote your income and labor to others, hate tyrants....

WALT WHITMAN (1819-1891)

The thing always happens
that you really believe in;
and the belief in a thing makes it happen.
And I think nothing will happen
until you thoroughly
and deeply believe in it.

FRANK LLOYD WRIGHT (1867-1959)

THE SECRET OF MAKING SOMETHING WORK IN YOUR LIFE IS,

FIRST OF ALL, THE DEEP DESIRE TO MAKE IT WORK:

THEN THE FAITH AND BELIEF THAT IT CAN WORK:

THEN TO HOLD THAT CLEAR DEFINITE VISION IN YOUR

CONSCIOUSNESS AND SEE IT WORKING OUT STEP BY STEP,

WITHOUT ONE THOUGHT OF DOUBT OR DISBELIEF.

EILEEN CADDY

Unless you give
yourself to some
great cause,
you haven't even
begun to live.

WILLIAM P. MERRILL

YOU MUST KNOW
FOR WHICH HARBOUR
YOU ARE HEADED
IF YOU ARE TO CATCH
THE RIGHT WIND
TO TAKE YOU THERE.

LUCIUS ANNAEUS SENECA
(C.55B.C.-C.40A.D.)

*A*nd when you come to a meeting of many ways

and do not know which to choose, do not choose at random,

but pause and reflect. Breathe with the trusting,

deep breaths you took when you first came into the world;

let nothing distract you, but wait and go on waiting.

Be still and listen in silence to your heart.

When it has spoken to you, rise up and follow it.

SUSANNA TAMARO, FROM "FOLLOW YOUR HEART"

Do not follow…

DO NOT FOLLOW

WHERE THE PATH MAY LEAD.

GO, INSTEAD,

WHERE THERE IS NO PATH

AND LEAVE A TRAIL.

AUTHOR UNKNOWN

It's the action,
not the fruit of the action,
that's important.
You have to do the right thing.
It may not be in your power,
may not be in your time,
that there'll be any fruit.
But that doesn't mean
you stop doing the right thing.
You may never know what results
from your action.
But if you do nothing,
there will be no result.

MAHATMA GANDHI (1869-1948)

One's lifework

One's lifework, I have learned, grows with the working
and the living. Do it as if your life depended on it,
and first thing you know, you'll have made a life out of it.
A good life, too.

THERESA HELBURN

No pleasure philosophy, no sensuality, no place nor power,
no material success can for a moment give such inner satisfaction
as the sense of living for good purpose.

MINOT SIMONS

*S*eek out that particular mental attitude
which makes you feel most deeply and vitally alive,
along with which comes the inner voice
which says, "This is the real me,"
and when you have found that attitude, follow it.

WILLIAM JAMES (1842-1910)

All that is necessary for the triumph of evil
is that good men do nothing.

EDMUND BURKE (1729-1797)

IT IS THE GREATEST OF ALL MISTAKES
TO DO NOTHING
BECAUSE YOU CAN ONLY DO LITTLE.

SYDNEY SMITH (1771-1845)

To know what is right and not to do it
is the worst cowardice.

CONFUCIUS (551-479 B.C.)

*O*ne does what
one must — in spite of
personal consequences,
in spite of obstacles
and dangers
and pressures —
and that is the basis
of all morality.

SENATOR JOHN F. KENNEDY
(1917-1963)

*We couldn't possibly
know where it would lead,
but we knew
it had to be done.*

BETTY FRIEDAN,
B.1921

You don't get to choose
how you're going to die.
Or when.
You can only decide
how you're going to live.
Now.

JOAN BAEZ, B.1941

BRAVE
HEARTS

I AM NOT AFRAID OF THE PEN,
OR THE SCAFFOLD,
OR THE SWORD.
I WILL TELL THE TRUTH
WHEREVER I PLEASE.

MOTHER JONES (MARY JONES)
(1830-1930)

It is hard to hold to integrity in times of terror —
yet some brave hearts have endured.

PAM BROWN, B.1928

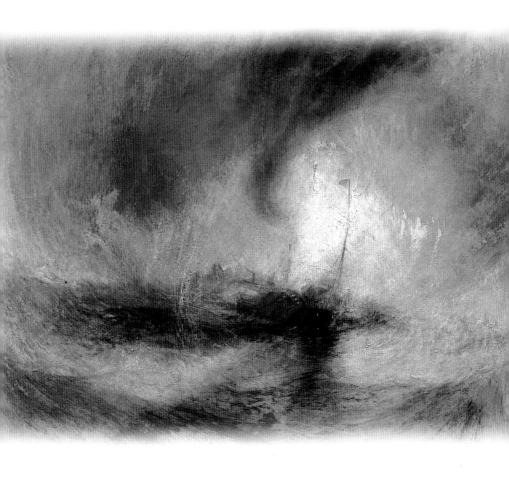

TRUE COURAGE IS NOT THE BRUTAL
FORCE OF VULGAR HEROES,
BUT THE FIRM RESOLVE OF VIRTUE
AND REASON.

ALFRED NORTH WHITEHEAD (1861-1947)

Whatever course you decide upon,
there is always someone to tell you
that you are wrong.
There are always difficulties arising
which tempt you to believe
that your critics are right.
To map out a course of action and follow it
to an end requires courage.

RALPH WALDO EMERSON (1803-1882)

We must not, in trying to think about how we can make a big difference, ignore the small daily differences we can make which, over time, add up to big differences that we often cannot foresee.

MARIAN WRIGHT EDELMAN, B.1939

If I have been of service,
if I have glimpsed more of the nature
and essence of ultimate good,
if I am inspired to reach wider horizons
of thought and action,
if I am at peace with myself,
it has been a successful day.

ALEX NOBLE

*Living in balance and purity
is the highest good for you and the earth.*

DEEPAK CHOPRA, B.1947

THE GREAT SPIRIT PLACED ME HERE...

TO TAKE GOOD CARE OF THE GROUND

AND TO DO EACH OTHER NO HARM.

YOUNG NATIVE AMERICAN

Guard within yourself that treasure, kindness. Know how to give without hesitation, how to lose without regret, how to acquire without meanness.

GEORGE SAND
(AMANDINE AURORE
LUCIE DUPIN)
(1804-1876)

The Sufis advise us to speak
only after our words
have managed to pass through three gates.
At the first gate, we ask ourselves,
"Are these words true?"
If so, we let them pass on;
if not, back they go.
At the second gate, we ask,
"Are they necessary?"
At the last gate, we ask,
"Are they kind?"

EKNATH EASWARAN (1911-1999)

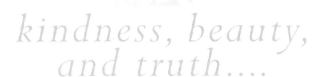

kindness, beauty, and truth....

THE IDEALS WHICH HAVE LIGHTED MY WAY,

AND TIME AFTER TIME HAVE GIVEN ME

NEW COURAGE TO FACE LIFE CHEERFULLY,

HAVE BEEN KINDNESS, BEAUTY, AND TRUTH....

THE TRITE SUBJECTS OF HUMAN EFFORTS —

POSSESSIONS, OUTWARD SUCCESS, LUXURY —

HAVE ALWAYS SEEMED TO ME CONTEMPTIBLE.

ALBERT EINSTEIN (1879-1955)

I think that the most significant work
we ever do, in our whole world,
in our whole life,
is done within the four walls of our own home.
All mothers and fathers,
whatever their stations in life,
can make the most significant of contributions
by imprinting the spirit of service
on the souls of their children,
so that the children grow up
committed to making a difference.

STEPHEN R. COVEY, PH.D

I vow to offer joy to one person in the morning
and to help to relieve the grief of one person
in the afternoon.
I vow to live simply and sanely, content with just
a few possessions, and to keep my body healthy.
I vow to let go of all worries and anxiety in order
to be light and free.

THICH NHAT HANH, B.1926

Do all the good you can,

By all the means you can,

In all the ways you can,

In all the places you can,

To all the people you can,

As long as ever you can.

JOHN WESLEY (1703-1791)

Find the journey's end in every step.

RALPH WALDO EMERSON (1803-1882)

If we are facing in the right direction,
all we have to do
is to keep on walking.

ANCIENT BUDDHIST EXPRESSION

EVERY TIME

YOU DON'T FOLLOW

YOUR INNER GUIDANCE,

YOU FEEL A LOSS

OF ENERGY,

LOSS OF POWER,

A SENSE OF

SPIRITUAL DEADNESS.

SHAKTI GAWAIN

A LIFE OF

Our great and glorious masterpiece
is to live appropriately.
All other things, to rule, to lay up treasure,
to build, are at most
but little appendices and props....

MICHEL DE MONTAIGNE (1533-1592)

VALUE

TRUTH IS THE ONLY SAFE GROUND TO STAND UPON.

ELIZABETH CADY STANTON
(1815-1902)

Truth is incontrovertible. Panic may resent it; ignorance may deride it; malice may distort it; but there it is....

SIR WINSTON CHURCHILL
(1874-1965)

CIVILIZATION IS FOUNDED ON INTEGRITY OF MIND AND HEART AND ACTION.

PAM BROWN, B.1928

If, for any reason whatsoever, moral standards
are conspicuously and unprecedentedly breached
in one area of society, such as the political,
it will follow as the night the day that those standards
will start collapsing all down the line —
in sports, entertainment, education, the armed forces,
business and government.

MARGARET HALSEY (1910-1997),
FROM "NO LAUGHING MATTER"

This above all:
to thine own self
be true.

WILLIAM SHAKESPEARE (1564-1616)

Everything's a circle.
We're each responsible for our own actions.
It will come back.

BETTY LAVERDURE, OJIBWAY

The most solid comfort one can fall back upon
is the thought that the business of one's life
is to help in some small way to reduce the sum of ignorance,
degradation and misery on the face of this beautiful earth.

GEORGE ELIOT (MARY ANN EVANS) (1819-1880)

A person who floats with the current, who does not guide themself according to higher principles, who has no ideal, no convictions — such a person is... a thing moved, instead of a living and moving being — an echo, not a voice....

HENRI FRÉDÉRIC AMIEL (1821-1881)

I've dreamt in my life dreams
that have stayed with me ever after,
and changed my ideas:
they've gone through and through me,
like wine through water,
and altered the colour of my mind.

EMILY BRONTË (1818-1848)

LIFE PRESENTS A NEVER ENDING SERIES
OF OPPORTUNITIES TO PERFORM ACTS OF CARING.
DON'T MISS EVEN ONE.

STUART AND LINDA MACFARLANE

smiles and
kindness

*Life is not made up of great sacrifices
and duties, but of little things;
in which smiles and kindness given habitually
are what win and preserve the heart.*

SIR HUMPHRY DAVY (1778-1829)

He has achieved success who has lived well,
laughed often and loved much;
who has enjoyed the trust and love of good people;
who has filled his niche and accomplished his task;
who has left the world better than he found it....

BESSIE A. STANLEY

You have to
count on living
every single day
in a way you believe
will make you feel
good about your
life — so that if it
were over tomorrow,
you'd be content
with yourself.

JANE SEYMOUR,
B.1951

THIS IS WHAT SETS THIS TINY OPAL OF A PLANET

OFF FROM A MILLION GREATER WORLDS

— THE POSSIBILITY OF KINDNESS

— THE POSSIBILITY OF CARE.

PAM BROWN, B.1928

A LIFETIME'S WORK

*A person's true wealth
is the good he or she does in the world.*

MOHAMMED (C.570-C.632)

When you look back on your life
and count your blessings
these will not be reckoned in terms of
money accumulated or rank achieved.
Instead what will prove to be most important
are the deeds you have done for others.

STUART AND LINDA MACFARLANE

WHAT AFTER ALL HAS MAINTAINED
THE HUMAN RACE ON THIS OLD GLOBE,
DESPITE ALL THE TRAGIC FAILINGS
OF MANKIND, IF NOT THE FAITH
IN NEW POSSIBILITIES
AND THE COURAGE TO ADVOCATE THEM?

JANE ADAMS

We can as individuals do so little to help the sad and suffering in the world — the lonely, bereaved, imprisoned, despised, exiled, sick in mind and body, the cold, the hungry.

Yet we can reach out to those within our knowledge, with courtesy and kindness, an unexpected gift, a visit.

Treating them with the respect that they deserve.

Honouring their courage. Listening to their stories.

For every kindness spreads in a shining circle: See how good people everywhere set rings of light moving across the darkness, rings that link and interlock.

PAM BROWN, B. 1928

ACKNOWLEDGEMENTS
The publishers are grateful for permission to reproduce copyright material. Whilst every reasonable effort has been made to trace copyright holders, we would be pleased to hear from any not here acknowledged. ROBERT FULGHUM: From *All I really need to know I learned in Kindergarten* by Robert L. Fulghum, copyright © 1986, 1988 by Robert L. Fulghum. Used by permission of Villard Books, a division of Random House, Inc. SHAKTI GAWAIN: Excerpted from *Awakening* by Shakti Gawain. Used with permission from New World Library, Novato, CA 94949, www.newworldlibrary.com. THICH NHAT HANH: Reprinted from *Call Me By My True Names: The Collected Poems of Thich Nhat Hanh* (1999) by Thich Nhat Hanh, with permission of Parallax Press, Berkeley, California, www.parallax.org. SUSANNA TAMARO: From *Follow Your Heart* © 1994 Baldini & Castoldi. Used with permission. PAM BROWN, STUART & LINDA MACFARLANE: published with permission © Helen Exley 2002.

LIST OF ILLUSTRATIONS
Exley Publications is very grateful to the following individuals and organizations for permission to reproduce their pictures. Whilst all reasonable efforts have been made to clear copyright and acknowledge sources and artists, we would be happy to hear from any copyright holder who may have been omitted.

Cover, title page and endpapers: *Morning*, S. KOSLOV, Scala

Page 6: *Study of an elm tree*, JOHN CONSTABLE, Scala

Pages 8/9: *Mountainous Landscape (oil on canvas)*, CASPAR DAVID FRIEDRICH (1774-1840), Hamburg Kunsthalle, Hamburg, Germany, Bridgeman Art Library

Page 11: *Rosa in un bicchiere*, MICHAIL VRUBEL, Scala

Pages 12/13: *Carolles (Manche)*, EMMANUEL LANSYER, Ann Ronan Picture Library

Pages 14/15: *Wintersonne am Niederrhein*, MAX CLARENBACH, Galerie Paffrath

Page 17: *Frühlingswiese*, MAX CLARENBACH, Galerie Paffrath

Page 18: *Lunchtime Preparations*, WILLIAM KAY BLACKLOCK, Fine Art Photographic

Page 20: *Livres et instruments de musique*, JAN VERMEULE, The Bridgeman Art Library

Pages 22/23: *Sonniger Wintertag*, MAX CLARENBACH, Galerie Paffrath

Page 25: *Untitled*, UNKNOWN ARTIST (20th Century), Ann Ronan Picture Library

Page 26: *The Timber Waggon*, JOHN ATKINSON GRIMSHAW, The Bridgeman Art Library

Page 28: *Morning Light, 1995 (pastel on paper)* ALICE DALTON BROWN (b. 1939), Private collection, Bridgeman Art Library. Courtesy Fischbach Gallery, New York

Page 31: *Woman sewing in the garden*, MARY CASSATT, The Bridgeman Art Library

Pages 32/33: *Panorama de Bruxelles*, JEAN DE LA HOESE, Belgian Pictures

Page 34: *Saint Loup - Parc du château*, EMMANUEL LANSYER, Ann Ronan Picture Library

Page 36: *Spring*, JAMES HERBERT SNELL, Fine Art Photographic

Page 38: *Les prairies à Giverny*, CLAUDE MONET, Ann Ronan Picture Library

Pages 40-41: *La Pie*, CLAUDE MONET, Ann Ronan Picture Library

Page 43: *Marine bleue près du bain des dames*, EMMANUEL LANSYER, Ann Ronan Picture Library

Page 44: *Sunrise, 1887*, GEORGE INNESS SNR (1825-1894), Brooklyn Museum of Art , New York, USA, Bridgeman Art Library

Page 47: *Field under a Stormy Sky*, VINCENT VAN GOGH, Ann Ronan Picture Library

Pages 48/49: *Vue du Canal St Martin*, ALFRED SISLEY, Ann Ronan Picture Library

Page 51: *Yellow Roses (oil on canvas)*, IGNACE HENRI JEAN FANTIN-LATOUR (1836-1904), Southampton City Art Gallery, Hampshire, UK, Bridgeman Art Library

Page 53: *The Moorish Kitchen Maid*, DIEGO RODRIGUEZ DE SILVA Y VELASQUEZ (1599-1660), National Gallery of Ireland, Dublin, Ireland, Bridgeman Art Library

Page 55: *Still Life with a Carpet Tablecloth c.1730*, RUSSIAN SCHOOL (18th Century), Hermitage, St.Petersburg, Russia, Bridgeman Art Library

Page 57: *Country Flowers, 1995 (oil on canvas)* OLEG ARDIMASOV (b.1936) Private Collection, Bridgeman Art Library

Pages 58/59: *La Luzerne*, GEORGES SEURAT, Ann Ronan Picture Library

Pages 60/61: *View across an extensive river valley*, DANIEL ESCOBAR (19th Century), Bonhams, London, UK, Bridgeman Art Library

Pages 62/63: *The Little Valley (panel)*, JEAN BAPTISTE CAMILLE COROT (1796-1875), Louvre, Paris, France, Bridgeman Art Library